table of contents

0 card – THE FOOL

The old name: Crocodile.

Archetype: child

3 -The astrological point: The air element; Uranium planet

4 – Kabbalistic equivalent:
Letter: Alef.

0 Arcana – THE FOOL (crocodile), takes No.0 either No.21 in the deck. Card itself shows a youngster, resolutely marching towards the rye. His moves are easygoing though he doesn't feel any happiness, only dilemma: which direction to choose. A dog, which symbolizes instincts and inconceivable feelings, is running beside him. The dog warns of possible danger. Mountains that are seen far-off show what distance Fool will have to face. White rose – sincerity, Venus and air symbol. The youngster meets the world. It's mystery what will happen next, whether he will stop or fall into the abyss. The card symbolizes some new opportunities. The youngster is searching for some life experience. Raspberry color of the feather denotes persistence and determination. Red – passion and impulsivity. He can't be taken as a fool, rather upcoming spring, Dionysus - the Greek God. Parcel – refusal of material goods, the four elements. Fool is the spirit and his parcel – information. Stick is like an experience which yet is not earned, it's information that is in youngsters hands though he doesn't know how to use it. Yellow color is the bond with the highest spheres;

also it is the symbol of the air element. Blue – sub consciousness. Mountains – obstacles, dangers. A dog denotes human's bestial nature and the five senses. White sun is the spring of life, the highest mind. Circles on a cloth of Fool symbolize the Sephirot. Eight spokes inside the circles symbolize spirit in the system of Hermetic Order of the Golden Dawn. Fool embodies birth, first steps, when there is no knowledge and experience, when trust is based on instincts and senses. Fool matches Uranium planet, air element, Aquarius sign. The planet is in charge of mental activity. Kabbalistic equivalent – letter Alev. Road eleven, according to chakras – first karmic card (there are four karmic cards).

Meanings

Card position "straight"

General meaning
Novelty, astonishment, turning over a new leaf, foolishness.
Disorder, chaos, foolishness, ignorance, failure.
Events
Beginning, risky steps, betrayal, new image.Nothing happens, stagnation, hesitation.

Business and work
Beginning of unknown activity, amateurism, eccentric business methods (circus, fair), unusual way of getting money.
Distraction, incompetence, particularly risky business.

Relationship
Spontaneous, new, romantic.   Vainglorious attitude, relationship is very superficial, vanishes in no time.
Health
Unusual illnesses, there is no fear of heights, careless attitude towards ones health, not diagnosed illnesses. Madness, mild psychological disorders, high risk of various traumas, especially head traumas.
Psychological characteristics
        Light-headed person, without any troubles, playful and joyful, loves life.   Apathetic,   foolishly naive, no self-

control.

Advise

To start from the beginning, to risk, do not be afraid, to step into uncertainty.

Do not start or do anything so far.

Warning

Shadow – irresponsibility, not to make risky moves and reckless actions.   Do not stop at the most important moment.

Result

Searching for the path, openness to innovations and the beginning of the new period.

Card turned upside-down

General meaning: Novelty, astonishment, turning over a new leaf, foolishness.Disorder, chaos, foolishness, ignorance, failure.

Events: Beginning, risky steps, betrayal, new image.Nothing happens, stagnation, hesitation.

Business and work: Beginning of unknown activity, amateurism, eccentric business methods (circus, fair), unusual way of getting money.   Distraction, incompetence, particularly risky business.

Relationship: Spontaneous, new, romantic.Vainglorious attitude, relationship is very superficial, vanishes in no time.

Health: Unusual illnesses, there is no fear of heights, careless attitude towards ones health, not diagnosed illnesses. Madness, mild psychological disorders, high risk of various traumas, especially head traumas.

Psychological characteristics: Light-headed person, without any troubles, playful and joyful, loves life.Apathetic, foolishly naive, no self-control.

Advise: To start from the beginning, to risk, do not be afraid, to step into uncertainty. Do not start or do anything so far.

Warning: Shadow – irresponsibility, not to make risky moves and reckless actions.Do not stop at the most important moment.

Result: Searching for the path, openness to innovations and the beginning of the new period.

You won't make a step, will be late, new period is not well-timed, you might stay for a fool.

You won't make a step, will be late, new period is not well-timed, you might stay for a fool.

Fool+The Magician – new job, new studies, younger and older brothers.

Fool + The High Priestess – young female lover, new feelings, unexpected victory, winnings.

Fool +The Empress – woman with a child.

Fool +The Emperor – father and a child, new position at work.

Fool +The Hierophant – family feast, minor help.

Fool +Lovers – new love, risky choice, thoughtless choice.

Fool +The Chariot – trip for the weekend, new car.

Fool +Strength – minor conflict.

Fool+Hermit – grandfather and grandson.

Fool +Wheel of Fortune – winnings in the lottery.

Fool +Justice – new conventions, alimony obtainment.

Fool +the Hanged Man – light condition of being drunk, late birth due date.

Fool +Death – crisis, caesarean section, minor traumas.

Fool +Temperance – unit piece of jewelry.

Fool +Devil – minor addiction.

Fool +Tower – new accommodation, minor accident, cloth damage.

Fool +Star – beginning of new love romance, birth.

Fool +Moon – childish fears.

Fool +Sun – child birth.

Fool +Judgement – family values, child's birthday.

Fool +World – journey abroad, emigration.

1 card – THE MAGICIAN

THE MAGICIAN.

1-The old name: illusionist.

2-Archetype: the creator, the heavenly Father.

3 – The astrological point: Mercury (God of an idea and communication).

4 – Kabbalistic equivalent: Letter: Beit.

.

Matches minor arcana's aces. Card depicts youngster with a raised up hand. The raised up hand denotes terrestrial origin's connection with cosmos and eternity. White shirt – purity of intentions, red toga – initiative, activeness. Belt consists of 2 wound snakes biting one's tails. It's the symbol of the eternity. In addition snake is god's Mercury's symbol. Circle symbolizes the eternal cycle of nature. Yellow is the color of the air element, Mercury symbolizes association with people, curiosity, friendliness. Planet Mercury is unstable, as quicksilver, and changes with respect to other planets with which it interacts. The messenger of the god Mercury receives and transmits information and often is the source of information itself. That is why The Magician distinguishes oneself with expressive speech, abilities for esoteric science. He invokes the highest forces and transforms them into material level. Lemniscate above The Magician's head – symbol of the eternity. It is bond with eternity as well as bond between human and God. There is a table in front of the The Magician. On it there are 4 elements which are symbols equivalent to 4 minor arcane parts. Square table symbolizes materiality. *Table with its four angles forms our life, The Magician knows how to realize everything what comes from elsewhere. He is able to use what nature has given him; at least he is learning how to use this gift.* Tools belonging to 4 rituals: goblet – receptive sphere of female, water – emotions; air – sword – thoughts, intelect, word, ability to communicate, speed, dynamics, difficulties, courage, person's intentions and aggression; scepter – fire, will, authority, acts, dynamics, manhood, origin, energetics; earth – coins – material needs, intention to use knowledge for own purposes. Scepter, goblet, sword and coin on the The Magician's table show that he knows how to use these all elements in order to reach one's goals. *To hold staff above one's head means ability to receive information from God and transfer it to earth.* White lilies denote purity of thoughts, good intentions, red roses – *heavenly love, wish, initiative.* In the wild nature bellflower, eglantine denotes intelligence, constant improvement. The card embodies cognition and reception of active male energy. But for her we can reach for the best result.

Meanings
Card position "straight"

General meaning: Quickness, initiative, resourcefulness, ability to persuade others, luck

Events: Loss, communication with siblings

Business and work: Authority, luck, resolute actions, volitional decisions, initiative employee, studies in the high school

Relationship: Fascination, affection.

Health: Pain, person might be in hospital or is visiting a clinic.

Psychological characteristics: Youthfulness, cognitive process, sociability, creative work, naturality. *Ability to concentrate without putting any effort.*

Advise: Believe in your abilities, abilities to deal with various problems, don't stop learning.

Warning: Shadow (the one inside) – liar, manipulator, charlatan

Result: Ability to control destiny, seek for ones goals, realize what is imagined

Card turned upside-down

General meaning: Fraud, destructive creation

Events: Anxiety, loss, rift with siblings, failure in the science field.

Business and work: Foolish initiative, inactivity, lack of will

Relationship: Shame.

Health: Mental illness or minor mental illnesses, problems with head, worthless treatment.
Psychological characteristics: Inconsistency, abnormal development, rigidity, rough intercourse.
Advise: Don't show volition, initiative.
Warning: You might meet a lack of will and consistency while realizing your plans
Result: Disability to finish work.

The Magician+The High Priestess – medicine sphere studies
The Magician+The Empress – older sister, personal business in beauty sphere
The Magician+The Emperor – new position at work
The Magician+The Hierophant– thesis or diploma defense
The Magician+Lovers – study choice, plans to move to a new job, relationship with relatives
The Magician+The Chariot – journey in order to visit relatives, car merchant
The Magician+Power – energetic treatment, fight between relatives, passionate relationship
The Magician+Hermit – older relative
The Magician+Wheel of Fortune – successful performance, time of negotiation
The Magician+Justice – formation of family juridical papers
The Magician+the Hanged – family disagreement, business stagnation
The Magician+Death – relationship breakdown
The Magician+Sequence – long realization of a plan
The Magician+Devil – hypnosis influence, borrowing from relatives
The Magician+Tower – job in the hospital, house division
The Magician+Star – successful actions, high grade mastery
The Magician+Moon – fear of taking any actions
The Magician+Sun – public appearance
The Magician+World – foreign relative arrival

2 card – THE HIGH PRIESTESS

THE HIGH PRIESTESS

    1 – The old name: Temple gates – Occult science on the threshold of the Isis Temple.

    2-Archetype: the mystery of female, virgin, Spiritual Bride and Mother.

    3 – The astrological point: Moon (hunt, chastity and goddess of virginity).

    4 – Kabbalistic equivalent:

Letter: Gimel.

. Wife of the The Hierophant, prophetess, queen of witches. Isis is a woman who is sitting between 2 columns and her face is covered with veil; Papessa (previous name of this card) – Joan the intelligent virgo *(according to the legend one girl named Joan was raised in the monaster where after some time she became The Hierophant. However when she became pregnant and everybody understood that she is a woman a new ritual turned up: before ordination to the The Hierophant, candidate must sit on the chair with no bottom and everybody have to be convinced of his manhood).* This card is guardian of the Taro, distinguishes by intuition, direct bond with God. Sorceress means passiveness, female energetic, symbolizes mystery and reticence. The High Priestess's crown is two half moons joined together and has a symbolic meaning of chastity, full moon denotes recurrence of existence. Shows whole Moon cycle.

Crown and veil – symbol of knowledge.

Moon's cycle symbolizes human soul, renunciation of passions.

Cross on the chest – connection of Egyptian male and female origins.

On the knees of The High Priestess there is a Torah scroll. It is the highest secret law, a book about the structure of the universe.

Two columns – black and white. Light and darkness, origins of manhood and femininity. Means there is no good without evil. One B (Bochaz), J (yiochin). These are columns which were built during the construction of Solomon's palace, and which have the connection with the Masonic Lodge.

The other name for the columns – temple gates. This is considered for Solomon's temple. The contrary balance between male and female creates a fight. The High Priestess doesn't stand out, equally assesses, doesn't give priority to anything emphasizing that two contraries will last for ever. A heavy curtain is between the columns – it is the curtain of ones who are not illuminated.

Embroideries with the palm branches denote the symbol of male origin and pomegranate fruits the symbol of female (fertility) origin (possible pregnancy). If The High Priestess's arcana falls out as a first card in the beginning of the oracle according to the majority of the professionals it is said that drawing lots is a useful thing to do. The The High Priestess embodies the passive female origin (number 2), which means patience and determination in order to obey to the higher leading power. She says that everything comes in its own time. She doesn't interrupt development of events but listens to the inner voice. The High Priestess's task is an expectation of an inner either external signal. She never interrupts. Moonlight isn't bright however it penetrates darkest corners transferring possibility to reveal the most confidential secrets.

'Yin' is the passive system of the world perception, we only observe and wait until the impulse to do something comes. The High Priestess teaches to go passive way through patience and expectation. It is the Eastern philosophy: to live in the harmony with nature, to go with the tide and trust ones inner voice that will tell when the time is right.

Card embodies the origin of the female, reception of the passive energy and comprehension of having it inside oneself. It also consolidates the principle of tolerance and comprehension that events can't be interfered.

Meanings

11

Card position "straight"

General meaning: Increased sensitivity, medium's abilities, and hidden factors.

Events: Surprising, unexpected changes of circumstances that were unlooked for, ability to keep secrets.

Business and work: Scientific work, book-keeping, economist, librarian, businessmen

Relationship: Mutual understanding, solicitude, idealization of a partner reason to a period of no sex, lover.

Health: Lives according to rhythm of nature, good health, vague symptoms.

Psychological characteristics: Consciousness: inner voice, mystery, reliability, ability to keep secrets.

Advice: Act according to inner voice, believe in intuition

Warning: Don't go with the tide waiting for a miracle; speak up when the moment is right.

Result: Merge with the former basis, go deep into oneself, pregnancy in the next two months, period – 40 days or a year.

Card turned upside-down

General meaning: Sullenness, garrulity, affection.

Events: Sudden and negative change, gossips, slanders.

Business and work: Affair managing without any plan and documentation, street work.

Relationship: Passion, loss of virginity, revenge.

Health: Exaggeration of endeavour, fear of nature and animals

Psychological characteristics: Superficial knowledge, garrulity, whimsicality, distrust in ones abilities.

Advice: Find solution to a problem, reveal a secret

Warning: Do not lose passiveness, don't destroy harmony

Result: Destruction of the harmony, voiceless intuition, erroneous view on the world structure.

The High Priestess+The Empress – birth of a new love romance
The High Priestess +The Emperor – verification of book-keeping documents, superior's lover
The High Priestess +The Hierophant – grandmother, family's secrets
The High Priestess +Lovers – secret lover, unexpected feelings, intuitive choice
The High Priestess +The Chariot – outing, beautiful car, unexpected journey
The High Priestess +Strength – dealing with the extrasensory practice

The High Priestess +Hermit – grandmother, solution to a raised question about pensions

The High Priestess +Wheel of Fortune – encounter with own destiny, unexpected winning

The High Priestess +Justice – work with the book-keeping documents

The High Priestess +the Hanged – crisis, forced disclosure of the information

The High Priestess +Death – crisis, lover becomes wife

The High Priestess +Sequence – diet

The High Priestess +Devil – inner fears, sex meetings

The High Priestess +Tower – flat renovation, *force major*

The High Priestess +Star – beauty contests, inner growth

The High Priestess +Moon – trip to the sea

The High Priestess+Sun – pregnancy, cosmetic procedures

The High Priestess+Judgement – unexpected meetings, valuable gifts

Sorcere+World – secret contacts, secret pregnancy

3 card –The The Empress

THE EMPRESS.

1-The old name: Isis-Uranium.

2-Archetype: Mother Nature, Heaven's and Earth's Daughter.

3 – The astrological point: Venus (goddess of love and feelings); period of puberty.

4 – Kabbalistic equivalent:

Letter: Dalet.

The Empress is sitting in the middle of the Blooming garden, garden – paradise, 12 stars on the crown denote 12 astrological signs. Heavenly nature is dependent on her. The other name – Isis or Urania. Is the symbol of heavenly wisdom. In her hands she has a scepter – symbol of power. A sphere on the scepter denotes symbol of globe. It is power, influence to the material world and symbol of Venus. Heart-shaped shield is leaned against the arm-chair. On it there is a sign 'o'with '+' that is the Venus sign. Shield and Venus symbolizes the feature of piece, love, beauty, solicitude. Those symbols repeat on her dress and this means protection of all those meanings. Garden is the symbol of paradise. Trees, wheat, flowers are the symbols of growth and fertility. The Empress is the material world surrounding human. She symbolizes female origin but in the concrete earthly manifestation that means everything what is natural and nature created. All stream-line forms symbolize endless cycle. Her task is giving birth and maintenance, preservation of something new. Denotes close relationship with children. Mistress suggests accepting oneself the way one is, to rely on fate. Keyword – I am doing. Corresponds to Minor Arcana's 3 (triplets). Planet – Venus. Element – earth and air. Kabbalistic equivalent: Dalet, in the Jewish alphabet Gimel. Gimel is the symbol of spiritual imagination in the material shell. This symbol occurs through the birth of the ideas and embodiment in all worlds: spiritual and material. On the right hand - eagle, the symbol of the sun or life, "the Holy Spirit". On the head of The Empress there is a crown that is decorated with 12 stars – 12 astrological signs. The heart-shape back of The Empress's arm-chair is the symbol of Venus. Twisting road round the The Empress, which goes over the boundaries of the garden, symbolizes secret that is known only to The High Priestess and will be revealed only to the holy one. Number 3 symbolizes Trinity, three-dimensional space. At first there was female Trinity: leda, lada, leta (childhood, youth, senility). Male: Zeus, Poseidon and Hades (heaven, water and inferno). Jupiter, Neptune, Uranium (Romanian Trinity). Number covers interest, assessment of "myself", bodily demands, stability and habits. Venus controls Aries and Libra.

meanings

Card position "straight"

General meaning: Growth,pregnancy,comfortable life, beauty, fertility, light, truth.

Events: Changes, achievement of unforeseen goal, controlling of the situation, luck.

Business and work: Creation work, design, cosmetology, manage a household, administration, legal open business, publicity.
Relationship: New acquaintance, ability to love and be loved, tenderness

Health: Living force, longevity.

Psychological characteristics: Consciousness: new perception

Advice: Seek for a rich soil, create family (marriage), act creative.
Warning: Avoid surplus however don't miss a chance.
Result: Life preservation and guardance.
Card turned upside-down

General meaning: Infertility,loss, lack of self confidence, loss of authority.

Events: Routine, solution of confused problems, folk festivals, doubtful hobbies and incomes.

Business and work: Unrevealed talents, lack of novelty, hackneyed solution.

Relationship: Pushed away love, loss of interest in the partner, infidelity, marriage break-up.

Health: Minor problems with health.

Psychological characteristics: anger, jammed into a corner.

Advice: Fight for luck, don't grudge own power.

Warning: Self-confidence only, roughness, stubbornness

Result: loss of authority

The Empress+The Emperor – wife and husband
The Empress +The Hierophant – family feast, women's consultation, bank storage
The Empress +Lovers – strong love, cosmetologist
The Empress +The Chariot – new car acquisition, meeting bringing about marriage, acquaintance with foreigner
The Empress+Strength – regained position, new love
The Empress +Hermit – long lasting loneliness
The Empress +Wheel of Fortune – fatal meeting, salvation of household questions, household chores
The Empress +Justice– signature of some documents related with children
The Empress +the Hanged – to be late, woman is forced to sacrifice her family
The Empress +Death – operation, property division
The Empress +Sequence – acquisition of the real estate
The Empress +Devil – acquisition of the real estate on credit
The Empress +Tower – isolation, divorce
The Empress +Star – cosmetology procedures, acquaintance with a beautiful person
The Empress +Moon – relaxation by the sea
The Empress +Sun – opening of a company, public appearance

The Empress +Judgement –giving birth, birthday
The Empress +World – beginning of long lasting relationship.

4 card THE EMPEROR

THE EMPEROR.

There is a man sitting on the throne. Throne is decorated with heads of Aries that is the symbol of the planet Mars and astrological sign of Aries.

Red gown and red sky are also the symbols of the element of fire and Mars; egyptian cross symbolizes life, the globe. The Emperor is a man in a relationship with the Empress, pillar in the house, financial sphere and in general plans. He is the master, ruler and sometimes even dictator, personification of authority, law and order.

1-The old name: cube-shaped stone, Osiris.
2-Archetype: Father who is consulting the world.
3 – The astrological point: Aries (vision). Spring – time of rapid growth and time of renewal of some actions.
4 – Kabbalistic euivalent:
Letter: Cheit.

meanings
Card position "straight"

General meaning: order, sequence, practical reason, stability, authority, cause, will

Events: Realization of some plans, visible result, space structuring

Business and work: Stable business, head of high rang, discipline, variety of market organizations and structural markets, state structures.
Relationship: strong, reliable, cherished, domination

Health: stable, not enough movement

Psychological characteristics: consciousness: realization of the ideas and intentions, logical analysis, practical conclusions, management

Advice: Realize your plans firmly and consistently

Warning: Stubborn severity, excessive pedantry and despotism can destroy feelings or live action
Result: Defense of reached results, guarantee of reliability and order.
Card turned upside-down

General meaning: immaturity, inability to control oneself

Events: Will never come true, collapsing of plans

Business and work: despotism, boredom, corruption, bad leadership, market collapse
Relationship: Obedience to alien power, goodwill, trust

Health: Addiction to alcohol or other drug

Psychological characteristics: A getaway from the reality, self-doubt, emotional outburst

Advice: Fight with disorganization and incompetence
Warning: Self-confidence only, roughness, stubbornness
Result: disregard of the authorities

The Emperor+The Hierophant – official of high position
The Emperor +Lovers – new creative project

The Emperor +The Chariot – business trip, new capacity

The Emperor +Strength – fight for a particular place, chief, headmaster

The Emperor +Hermit – manager of the insurance company, elderly man

The Emperor +Wheel of Fortune – routine at work

The Emperor +Justice – sittings of the Judgement, signature of business-like documents

The Emperor +the Hanged –loss of position, changes of business strategy

The Emperor +Death – bankruptcy, situation of crisis

The Emperor +Temperance – a stable situation, long-term job

The Emperor +Devil – bank employee

The Emperor +Tower – official of high rank, divorce and property division

The Emperor +Star – promising position, beautiful person

The Emperor +Moon – connections, money "washing", infidelity with the manager

The Emperor +Sun – known person

The Emperor +World – transnational character

5 card – THE HIEROPHANT

THE HIEROPHANT

The first priest is shown in the card dressed in The Hierophant's tiara, and sitting on the throne between two columns, blessing two people either two travelers. Dark traveler's clothes are the symbol of soul that has traveled enough around the world. This is very alike to the bible story 'prodigal son'. Traveler with the light clothes symbolizes soul that has just started its journey, is inexperienced, pure, and may act unpredictable.

If The Emperor is the representative of material authority, then The Hierophant represents spiritual authority. The Hierophant attracts into the spiritual world, comforts, hears out, turns one's thoughts, gives advice, blesses before journey. He can be considered as an indirect guardian of those whose career is related with communication with other people. In Christianity his image is close to image of Saint Nicholas (cleric who hears out confessions).

1-The old name: the Master of Arcanum.
2-Archetype: God's vicar, sait, Tutor.
.
3 – The astrological point: Taurus (hearing).
4 – Kabbalistic equivalent:
Letter: Vav.

meanings

Card position "straight"

General meaning: Conservative attitude, good advice, education (highest most common), family, clan, kin, religion, tradition

Events: Implied subject, obtainment of valuable advice, marriage, christening, religious and family values and feasts

Business and work: Folk craft, hereditary professions, business that requires traditional attitude, old-fashioned attitude, taking into account the human factor at work

Relationship: Legal marriage, Church marriage, union, traditional relationship as parental, constant, time-tested, family blessed

Health: Regular standard procedures or methods of treatment, old-fashioned treatment using verified tools

Psychological characteristics: Consciousness: search of meaning of life and discovering, authority, sensible, fair

Advice: Ask for an advice from sage, authoritative people; act as usual, as admissible

Warning: Don't be too proud of what you have achieved, never be a fanatic of truth, don't listen to wrong advices

Result: Deep inner trust in oneself as the result of belief in the highest aim

Card turned upside-down

General meaning: Unusual solution to a problem, non-standard attitude

Events: experiment, inadequate behavior willingness to act according to unchecked methods, refusal of advices

Business and work: Counterfeiting of religious goods and antique, loss of traditional technologies and recipes

Relationship: cohabitation, non-traditional relationship, a scandal in the family that respects traditions, inconstant homosexual relationship

Health: Latest or experimental methods of treatment, attempt to treat oneself using untraditional methods, violation of normal state

Psychological characteristics: weakness, too much of kindness, immorality, no conscience, criminal or false authority

Advice: Listen to nobody, act on the contrary to traditions, break boundaries

Warning: Threat that traditional attitude won't be followed, a threat of conflict between children and their parents, you might get into a wrong influence under some religion or tradition
Result: extreme, non-traditional solution in the traditional situation, disregard of the authorities

The Hierophant+Lovers – a loving family, choice between family and beloved one
The Hierophant+The Chariot – growth of authority, journey in order to visit relatives
The Hierophant+Strength – fight in the family, authority, prophet
The Hierophant+Hermit – the older member of the family, manager of the insurance company, teacher
The Hierophant+Wheel of Fortune– successful consultation, timely help
The Hierophant+Justice – lawyer
The Hierophant+the Hanged – spiritual crisis
The Hierophant+Sequency – teacher in the teaching institution, family of strong bond
The Hierophant+Death – divorce, separation
The Hierophant+Devil – professional adviser
The Hierophant+Tower – politician of great importance, divorce
The Hierophant+Star – searches of meaning, programmer-consultant
The Hierophant+Moon – deception in the family, infidelity
The Hierophant+Sun – famous adviser, recognition in the society
The Hierophant+World – transnational character of great importance

6 card – LOVERS

1-The old name: two paths
2-Archetype : choice,Eros
3- The astrological point: Gemini
4-Kabbalistic egualent: Letter Zayn

A man and a woman are depicted in the card. Archangel Raphael is gliding above their heads. According to the legend it was Raphael who brought a magical ring with engraving of mightypower hexagon star to the king Solomon who used this ring and symbol in order to control demons.

Behind the lovers there is the Tree of Knowledge of Good and Evil with 5 red apples denoting 5 ways of knowledge that we understand as Universal ways of life. According to the Bible the Tree of Knowledge of Good and Evil is an extraordinary tree that was planted by God in the middle of the Eden garden. Symbolizes knowledge, especially ethical, ability to make a right choice between Good and Evil. Behind the man there is a life tree with 12 flaming trifoliates symbolizing 12 astrological signs.

Woman is gazing at the archangel, and the man is looking at woman because the angel voice can be heard only by the woman.

Meanings
Card position "straight"

General meaning: Right choice, partnership, attraction, love, beauty

Events: Suggestion to choose, gathering with the choice, solution to the awkward situation

Business and work: advertisement, beauty industry, marriage agencies, work one is fond of, matured project
Relationship: The joy of communication, clarity of the choice, admission, unity, blessed from above

Health: Well-being depends on the spiritual state, well-being after the proper selection of treatment

Psychological characteristics: Understanding of ones individuality, ability to adopt the right decision

Advice: Find a common language with a partner, make up ones mind, show oneself
Warning: Do not rush to make a choice, fear of double-dealers, indecision, choice might be wrong
Result: Merge of oppositions. You shall make up your mind and choose wisely, you will choose love

Card turned upside-down

General meaning: Wrong choice, being late, infidelity

Events: Marriage collapse, end of love, divorce/separation, situation without a way out

Business and work: Show business, disliked job, black technologies
Relationship: Unreliable relationship between partners, sorrow, inability to improve relationship, divorce/separation, trauma of former communications, inability to trust

Health: problems, inappropriate treatment, bad well-being, slowly developing processes, veneral diseases

Psychological characteristics: Inability to solve problems, wandering around

Advice: Choice refusal, let the circumstance make the decision
Warning: Difficulties while adopting the solution; too slow adoption of the decision

Result: Solution will not be accepted, solution can be wrong

Lovers+The Chariot – right choice, determined marrying
Lovers+Strength – choice made under the pressure
Lovers +Hermit – one who can love only one person
Lovers +Wheel of Fortune – unforgettable relationship
Lovers +Justice – official registration of a relationship
Lovers +the Hanged – forced choice, unwished choice
Lovers +Death – end of the infidelity
Lovers+Temperance – living with two families, decision that requires some time
Lovers +Devil – sexual seductions
Lovers +Tower – divorce/separation
Lovers +Star – new love, creative project, exhibitions
Lovers +Moon – fear to make a choice
Lovers +Sun – happy relationship, public relationship
Lovers +World– foreign partner

7 card – CHARIOT

1-The old name: Osiris's The Chariot.

2-Archetype: beginning of feats, solution, escape to the outer world.

3 – The astrological point: Cancer (speech).

4 – Kabbalistic equivalent:

Letter: Cheit.

Card depicts wagoner riding a Chariot with the harnessed sphinxes. White sphinx symbolizes the energy of good, black – destructive energy, uncertainty, force which hinders to achieve the goal. Sphinx is the guardian of the holy wisdom and the secret; one that keeps the harmony between active and passive energy. The canopy in the Chariot is embroidered with stars that symbolize outer space. The Chariot's front has a tantric symbol denoting huge creating energy. Two stones that are on the wagoner's shoulders - Urim and Thummim, allow to understand any language of the world. His belt is decorated with Zodiac signs and 12 holy stones.

Beginning of a journey towards new goal. White sphinx – clarity, purity, everything what is positive and energetic. Black sphinx – destructive energy, energies that stop development and journey towards the particular goal. Important aspect: wagoner controls both of these powers and tries to suppress them while achieving one or another goal.

Victory does not come easily. This card means victory but only if we are able to resist the temptations depending from the greatness of the goal. City behind is the conquered city. Journeys, move to a new place, trip to a foreign country are coming up. Usually sevens do not live in the motherland or travel much. A lot of energy, though it is hard for a person to form own goals.

Previously a coffin was showed in this card. Immediately after the coffin three crying women follow; that's why sometimes The Chariot may denote funeral (though this information can't be known to a client), undertaker's office.

For a person there will always be a conflict between a family and career, self-realization.

Meanings
Card position "straight"

General meaning: courage, self-confidence, desire of new experiences, luck, career, businessman's spirit, wish to risk, popularity, war, triumph, revenge

Events: Journey, triumph, glory, journey to the foreign country, parcel delivery

Business and work: New job or position, own business; business-trips, transport, drivers, transportations, car marketing
Relationship: New acquaintance, new stream; dynamic, sweet relationship, tending towards consolidation, bright, fortunate

Health: Recovery, great health, victory against the illness

Psychological characteristics: Self-confidence; bent for aggression, very strong extrasensory, strong intuition, troubles with working in group, work from 8 to 17 constrains them a lot, any restriction. People of this kind have to know the final goal, and decide themselves the form of achievement

Advice: Take control of affairs without any delay or second thought Trust in oneself and ones forces
Warning: If you don't know how to do it – don't do it at all
Result: „treasure discovery, liberation of a beauty", aggressive relationship will lead to marriage, new work during the journey, aim will be reached quicker through a journey
Card turned upside-down
General meaning: defeat, stagnation, captivity, end of luck, end of popularity, evil fame

Events: Rough and unsafe movement, sluggish, attack, an elephant in a crystal shop, stopping, loss, failed trip

Business and work: Unsuccessful risk, temporary stopping during the development process, unwillingness, suspended journey, risk of an accident

Relationship: Stopped sequence of events, break ups, relationship leading nowhere, attempt to make them better make only worse

Health: Disappointment in the treatment, hypodynamia, bed rest necessity, apathy, condition with no changes

Psychological characteristics: Fear of criticism, its better not to stand out, one who can't refuse or very cruel despot

Advice: Be more modest; the calmer you drive the further you get
Warning: Fear of rough actions from an ambush and loss of the control of situation
Result: Refusal to go further, inadequate modesty or rudeness as a defensive reaction

The Chariot+Strength – new relationship, sultry way of searching for a solution during the conflict
The Chariot +Hermit – permanent business trip
The Chariot +Wheel of Fortune – periodic trips, determined and fortune car purchase
The Chariot +Justice – official registration of a vehicle, examination of papers in the road
The Chariot +the Hanged – car breakdown, be delayed on the trip, river transport driver
The Chariot +Death – breakdown on the road, extreme journey, skiing
The Chariot+Sequence –long-term journey
The Chariot+Devil – theft of a vehicle or a breakdown
The Chariot+Tower– car accident, dismissal from office, soldier
The Chariot +Star – marriage, long-awaited proposal
The Chariot+Moon – cruise, trip to the sea
The Chariot +Sun – reaching for recognition
The Chariot+World – trip to the foreign country, emigration

8 card – THE STRENGTH

1-The old name: tamed lion.

2-Archetype: wild power, battle with the Dragon.

3 – The astrological point: Lion (taste) – love and wise diversion of will

4 – Kabbalistic equivalent:

Letter: Teit – „fur for wine", simple letter that matches Lion.

Card depicts girl who is pressing lion's jaws. White dress denotes purity, spiritual strength. Green is the colour of tranquility that distinguishes with good intuition, has congenital power of treatment and wish to help others. Green stimulates sense of touch, increases harmony with oneself, reduces stress, increases fertility, energy. Red flowers – intelligence and obedience to divine law (on the head and round the waist). Girl and lion symbolize the fight of two divine origins: it is a positive creative energy, love and animal instincts. She tempers the lion and shows this way that it is better to control rather then to destroy. Symbol of infinity is the rising above the material world. Tenacity adorns woman and allows her to gently temper the lion. Lion isn't aggressive, the tail is shoved and four paws rest upon the ground. Lion symbolizes unconscious instincts and force that will have to be controlled in order to curb the destructive power. While fighting with the negative factors it is necessary to rely on the strength of feelings rather than physical strength. It is the power of love because only love can win over the rage; it is the power of unity. Plait of roses denote the power of good intentions, wishes and it is the power to which any force that cannot apprehend oneself cannot fight it. The infinity symbol represents power and whoever perceives that sign is unstoppable.

Card shows particular stage of life of a person when it becomes necessary to curb one's human passions and emotions, however this has to be done gently with love and percept of one's inherent essence rather then done using the rough force.

Meanings
Card position "straight"

General meaning: courage, vitality, energy, interest, authority, great opportunities, action, endurance

Events: Force situation to obey to ones will, show power of ones anger or untimely wishes, right actions

Business and work: energetic, power structures, main companies, power, the leading link, conveyor, organization of the thesis, luck
Relationship: passion, implementation of wishes, strong bright feelings, one person subordinate to another, drama, for a man – open passion, for woman - sex

Health: Great various energetic practice and self-regulation, person can defeat illness with his own strength

Psychological characteristics: Consciousness: original thinking, rapidness of thinking, charisma; will, self-confidence, knows how to use ones abilities

Advice: Show up, prepare for a battle, totally devote to a favorite job, affair or beloved

Warning: Extreme pitch awaits for you; don't overestimate one forces, don't break down; don't use only force
Result: Perception and transformation of low incentive, you shall reach your aim

Card turned upside-down

General meaning: irresponsibility,   abuse of power, relationship problems, weakness

Events: Work not according to the strength, uncontrollable situation, inhumane acts, aggression

Business and work: Inability to control, uncontrollable ploy, accidents in the large objects, irresponsibility, cruelty of the business development methods', price competition

Relationship: Tired from a constant fights in a relationship, lack of interest in a relationship, coolness in the sensibilities, recession, cruelty, conflict with oneself, conflict with the family

Health: Illness has won, helplessness, muscle sprain, tendon breakdown, blood pressure spikes, karmic illnesses, ones health manipulation

Psychological characteristics: Suspicious uncontrollable fears, can be psychological either physical victim of abuse, diffident, coward

Advice: Don't go va bank, refrain, show sage fear, „assume", be diplomat

Warning: Blind fury that can lead to explosion; ambitions of a million and the result is worth only 1 cent; you may lose the battle

Result: Comprehend or not (voluntary or involuntary) misunderstandings, shame, weakness in the situation, situation will reveal your blind spots

Strength + Hermit – powerful manager, owner of the personal enterprise
Strength+Wheel of Fortune – fatal events
Strength+Justice – fight in the Judgment, official registration of a relationship
Strength+the Hanged – increased pressure, inner crisis
Strength+Death – physical injuries
Strength+Sequence – life in a harmony, diet
Strength+Devil – physical addiction, drug addiction or drunkenness
Strength+Tower – physical injuries
Strength+Star – spiritual growth, beginning of a permanent relationship
Strength+Moon – physical ailment, inherent fears
Strength+Sun – occupation of the high capacity, gymkhana

Strength+Judgement – renewal of a relationship
Strength+World – receipt of a recognition, smooth journey

9 card – THE HERMIT

THE HERMIT.

Card depicts an elderly person wearing a monk's habit and standing on the top of the mountain. It denotes symbol of age. Though it is the night and landscape is dark it is not bleak; means that the right time came for withdrawing from an active career; time of meditation. Hermit does not suggest us to reject exterior world however to take a good peer into the inner world. A person with the monk's wear is standing on the top of the mountain (it is believed that it is a middle-aged fool). In his raised hand there is a lantern – the light of reason that has a shining star in it denoting justified expectations. Lantern symbolizes constant vigilance. The light of this lantern sheds light on his past, present and future. A bat is an inner power, spine, because bat is divided into 7 parts with springs denoting inner awareness which is his only anchor. Lantern's star is the astrological sign of Virgo which means "servant of the people". Cape is the tool of sage allowing him to feel alone even in the rabble. His ability is to hide his secret, keep silent and act in the silence. Beard and cape symbolizes the compability of male's and female's origins. Bat also is the symbol of phallus denoting human's consciousness. It also shows knowledge, experience that can be fallen back on.

The Hermit is standing on the top of the mountain and covers all the view which means that he can perfectly see his future perspectives. This way the Hermit shows that it is necessary to find strength in oneself so that you could rise above the situation and calmly think about it. A bat is also necessary – it husbands the energy. Hunched up from the work and concerns however calm. Eyes are closed so he could see the light of truth. He doesn't need earthly sight. The inner light in his heart guides him. Sage is an allegory. This card symbolizes the search of spiritual wealth and going deep into inner world as well as balance, carefulness, inner concentration, sometimes points out loneliness and isolation from the life. In common parlance card is named the Monk. You can't find disappointment in this card, the inner concentration of the Hermit is the concentration in order to reach the final aim. First of all the appearance of the Hermit in the puzzle means level of self-control. Hermit's card shows that we can assess oneself as a character. In addition, person has to show and transmit through experience and knowledge.

1-The old name: suspended lamp.
2-Archetype: inner guide, the old Sage.
3 – The astrological point: Virgo (junction).
4 – Kabbalistic equivalent:

Meanings
Card position "straight"

General meaning: Loneliness, asceticism, going out from the world to oneself, esoteric, wisdom, reticence.

Events: Presence in the solitude, cogitations, getting deep into oneself, concentration, independent actions

Business and work: Personal enterprise, own business path, inner reserves, decrease in the production losses, unique craft experts, elaborate business, custom work, piece articles
Relationship: loner, difficult relationship, no emotions, long solitude, widowhood, love to only one person.

Health: Pay close attention to the bones, spine and state of mind (spirit)

Psychological characteristics: Consciousness: freedom from the alien attitude system; learning from the mistakes of others, elderly person

Advice: Go your own way, become yourself, stay alone for a while, follow doctor's advices

Warning: Shadow: putting too much emphasis on something, gloominess, anger, do not isolate oneself from the outer world, satisfaction of oneself and environment
Result: Go your own way, be yourself, do not rush

Card turned upside-down

General meaning: Undue insurance, interest in the outer world, isolation,inability to understand obious matters; fear

Events: Exiting the shadow, end of solitude, false reticence, inability to stay in solitude

Business and work: inadequacy of the market, necessity to start mass production, business out of order, non-demanded goods
Relationship: Widowhood „shallow" relationship, solitude has to end soon

Health: Unwillingness to see the cause of an illness, the ambiguity of the diagnosis, endless worries due to illness

Psychological characteristics: Unfounded prudence, fear of solitude, fears, complex of low self-assessment

Advice: Hide, disguise yourself

Warning: Avoid frivolous attitude towards the work, self-underestimation, violence of personal space
Result: Start your own way, listen to thyself, search of new paths to reach people

Hermit+Wheel of Fortune – encounter after a long solitude
Hermit +Justice – long-term agreements
Hermit +the Hanged – forced solitude
Hermit +Death –crisis, drunkenness, life-threatening combination
Hermit +Sequence – permanent solitude, work of one capacity
Hermit +Devil – permanent addiction to drugs and alcohol, long-term credit
Hermit +Tower – house construction, credits, imprisonment, hospital
Hermit +Star – finding of a purpose
Hermit +Moon – business trip for a month
Hermit +Sun – going out
Hermit +Judgment – inheritance receipt

Hermit + World – going out across the world, business-trip to the foreign country

10 card – WHEEL OF FORTUNE

WHEEL of FORTUNE.

Matches tenth Minor Arcana.

Element – fire. Symbolics – Circle of Time (kalachakra Tantra). The Yin and Yang circle is the circle of life and death. Thick clouds and violet sky denotes Jupiter. The violet colour means going deep into spiritual matter, humanitarian activity. It denotes attraction to ones who need help. Negative qualities: inability to say "no", inability to take a rest. This colour also provides time perception, controls consciousness, carries out the thought control.

Hermanubus (shape of the human with the jackal's head) one of the manifestations of Hermes.Typhon with the initial snake's reflection and demon Hermanubus symbolizes alchemical mercury, susceptibility, stream. Typhon is the symbol of salt denoting inertia.

Sphinx – sulfur – energy, activity.

Shiva –destroyer, Vishnu – guardian, Bahma – creator.

In the corners there are 4 animals of Ezekiel. 4 angels two rubies, depicting The Chariot of heavenly Ezekiel's. Circle matches Ezekiel's vision (Bible) mentioned by Levis.

Circle symbolizes the continuity of the life cycle but at the same time it reminds that life is composed from the whole of various cycles changing one another.

Circle has a centre that symbolizes our individuality. It is our inner world that has a necessary fulcrum within. Precisely here the wheel is attached though it seems that it is moving freely in the space.

The outer side of the wheel is the existing world with which we are constantly in contact. Spokes are the energy channels where the energy of "I"flows and is able to contact the world it is surrounded by. Rotating wheel was also imagined as a woman. She is on duty at the blindly rotating wheel because by chance wheel can be turned to good or bad. Sometimes she is not blind but blindfolded that symbolizes coincidence of her decision. When card has 4 shapes of people in it then person on the top of the wheel has the authority and person's going down the wheel days are counted. Underneath you don't have any authority however chances change with each step taken up; it is the ups and downs of life. Eternal movement of the wheel is uncontrollable. Wheel of Fortune is a weird combination of destiny and free will. Destiny is linked with the moving part of the wheel, stable hub and symbolizes truth. Tetragram on the letter on the wheel is the name of the God: TORA, TARO, ROTA (raph).Letters of the Jewish alphabet.

Tetragram – 4 letters. Alchemical symbols – formula of cyclicality

1 – formation
2 – existence
3 – disappearance
Anubis, Sphinx, Set
Taurus – earth – spring
Lion – fire – summer
Eagle – water – autumn, scorpion
Angel – air – aquarius

Signs and symbols on the wheel show the existence of the mysterious laws of the universe. There are 3 aspects of human on the wheel. On the left – snake (symbol of destruction). On the right – Anubis who is watching at the sky where he is heading at. On the top there is a sitting sphinx with a sword. He controls the wheel, balances the symbols of good and evil embodies destiny. He allows wise ones to rise and tears down prigs. In the four corners of the card there are 4 shapes denoting 4 elements, 4 seasons, astrological signs. All figures have books. That means "acknowledge me" (God), natural laws, tasks and lessons of the destiny. Four creatures guard the God's throne. Lion – priority, kingship, Taurus – prey. Figure with human face – God's son. Eagle is the Holy Spirit. Moral sense. Human's face enforces thinking. Lion – courage, Taurus – not giving in to pleasures of the world, eagle – to watch at the sky and rise as the Christ. Saint Matthew – human's head, John the Apostle – eagle, Saint Marc – lion, Saint Luke – Taurus. It is card of good changes and good signs, beginning of the new and fortunate cycle or life. Symbol of oneself and everything's improvement. Everything is circling, there is nothing constant except the universe.

It is the circle of time. Card shows that circle of time brings new events, new matters to this life. Everything what is old becomes obsolete and goes away. Renewal.

1-The old name: Sphinx.
2-Archetype: destiny.
3 – The astrological point: Jupiter God of love, fortune and prosperity).
4 – Kabbalistic equivalent:
Letter: Kaf – „palm"

Meanings
Card position "straight"
General meaning: Key decisions and actions, awards and opportunities, fortune, destiny grace, individual karma, events

Events: Unexpected changes or events, fluke, whirl of events, fortune

Business and work: bazaar, market, high turnover, great orders, fast profit, gambling business, seasonal business, business, dependent on natural factors, routine
Relationship: It's destiny, sudden, bright, memorable

Health: Unexpected illnesses, fast recovery, epidemics

Psychological characteristics: Consciousness: perception of the Supreme Law, calmly accepts what destiny sends
Advice: Acknowledge your destiny, allow to happen what is meant, talk to occultists, use the opportunity
Warning: Do not be a fatalist, don't stop, don't wait for the grace of the fate
Result: Transformation from the lowest to the highest; period of luck
Card turned upside-down
General meaning: Recession, negative karma, luck loss, delay, disturbing, the collapse of the old problems

Events: Repeated recession, repetitive events, failure, daily worries, losses

Business and work: Stagnation of affairs, failure, untimely start, stop of turnover or decrease of its level, old goods and the impossibility to realize them.

Relationship: The end is coming up, there is no motion in the development of a relationship

Health: Slow recovery, fears, power recession

Psychological characteristics: Repetition of the old mistake, inability to see positive things, destructive thinking

Advice: Learn to see positiveness in any situation
Warning: shadow: fatality, loss of the fire of life, fear of tomorrow
Result: Period of various events, it's better to pay attention to them

Wheel of Fortune+Justice – winning of the Judgment
Wheel of Fortune +the Hanged – hard times
Wheel of Fortune +Death – natural disasters
Wheel of Fortune +Temperance– sequence of neutral events
Wheel of Fortune +Devil – winning in the lottery or casino, dependency from the outer situation
Wheel of Fortune +Tower – long-term imprisonment, work in a state institution
Wheel of Fortune +Star – lucky incident
Wheel of Fortune + Moon –flood, periodic fears
Wheel of Fortune + Sun – office occupation, trip to the resort
Wheel of Fortune +Judgment – revival of the past relationship, meeting with an old friend
Wheel of Fortune +World – emigration

11 card – JUSTICE

Karmic card

1 –The old name: Themis, Libra and sword.
2-Archetype: destiny.
3 – The astrological point: Libra (action, work).
4 – Kabbalistic equivalent:
Letter: Lamed, „hornlet".

Card depicts woman in the throne between two columns with a sword in one hand – it's the truth and scales that symbolize harmony in the other hand. She symbolizes impartiality. It is goddess Dike who symbolizes justice. Her eyes aren't tied because it is divine justice that is able to see everything. Two columns: one is column of mercy, second is the column of strict retribution or punishment. Eyes are wide open so that the goddess of justice could make conclusions about what is good and what is bad.

Covering is the line between what can be seen and what is unseen.

Libra is the balance and even the least fuzz can counterbalance the plate. All actions will be weighted.

Sword is the weapon, authority, law, symbol of punishment, strict retribution. Sword to the top denotes punishable justice that protects good and punishes evil.

Libra and sword – the dual essence of justice, precision and rigor, symbol of the spiritual balance.

The old name – Themis, second name – „sword and scales".

This is the card of racional and logical thinking.

Sword and scales mean that it is necessary to weigh the circumstances. Columns denote sides of circumstances that have to be taken into account. Be honest with yourself. One column is Yin, another Yang. Evaluation how harmonious we are.

Meanings
Card positon "straight"

General meaning: equality, truth , general occurrence of law primacy (justice) , maintenance, clarity, wise decision

Events: Confronting with the consequences of the previous actions, positive solution, award reception, litigation

Business and work: Law enforcement agencies, contractual obligations, penalties, damage compensation, receipt according to merits, antimonopoly laws, equal competitive conditions, divorce and wealth division. Correct distribution of money. Solving juridical issues dealing with property and money, fortune will be on your side, because justice is on your side. In some cases monetary compensation will have to be paid. Try to get money trough honest means.

 At work as never you will need honesty, endurance and orderliness. It is necessary to divide work and responsibility to equal parts. Problems solved, tension slackened

Relationship: equality, the balance of power, calm, legitimize, official divorce and wealth division, harmony, attraction to opposite type person

Health: Result of improper lifestyle and bad habits, formal diagnosis, specific diagnosis

Psychological characteristics: Consciousness: sober, practical approach, considering solutions, objective self-assessment, inner principles, person having business-like abilities, mature and experienced person

Advice: To look soberly and objectively at an affair, responsibly
Warning: Avoid preconception and formalism

Result: Objective knowledge, thoughtful approach, reception according to merits (not more not less), you shall make a formal agreement, try to acquire balance in all areas of life

Card turned upside-down

General meaning: injustice, predestination, surfeit, disbalance

Events: Incorrect verdict, troubles with the document formation, criminal case, loss of honor, injustice

Business and work: Problems with education, antipode between work and relaxation, belief in infallibility, injustice, default, judicial mistakes

Relationship: fate, injustice, disharmony, karma, that was meant to be, distrust, no feelings, envy , constant control

Health: Health aggravation, wrong diagnosis

Psychological characteristics: Antipode of mind and feelings, unfair self-assessment, suspicion, fear, feeling of guilt, fear of being punished for sins

Advice: Listen to your soul's wish to grow and change, free yourself from preconception, don't judge and you won't be judged
Warning: You don't believe in your rightness, you lack inner power
Result: Undue resentment, disharmony, punishment, collision of works and plans, time of great challenges

Justice+The Fool – alimony, defeat in the Judgement
Justice +The Magician – education at the Faculty of Law, successful official registration of some documents
Justice +The High Priestess – accounting records, delayed decision
Justice +The Empress – successful defense, company establishment, management of documents related to children
Justice +The Emperor – official, judge, Judgment, notarial document registration
Justice +The Hierophant – lawyer, legal advice
Justice +Lovers – right decision, official registration of a relationship, Palace of Marriages
Justice +The Chariot – car purchase, fines for violation of the rules
Justice +Strength – battle in the Judgment, won case
Justice +Hermit – experienced lawyer, long process
Justice +Wheel of Fortune – fortunate document signing, timely registration
Justice +the Hanged – defeat, forced signing of the contract

Justice +Death– end of the trial

Justice +Temperance – long process of the registration of the real estate

Justice +Devil – deceptive contract

Justice +Tower – imprisonment, judicial proceedings, purchase/sell of the real estate, divorce

Justice + Star – a fateful decision

Justice +Moon– fraud with documents

Justice +Sun – marriage contract, fortunate contracts

Justice +Judgment – official legacy registration

Justice +World – official registration of the real estate

12 card – THE HANGED MAN

1-The old name: victim, drowned person.

2-Archetype: victim, captivity.

3 – The astrological point: water element (planet Neptune – God of the Sea).

4 – Kabbalistic equivalent:

The Hanged man is hung up on a cross-beam (tree). The cross-beam is a Tau cross (last letter of Scandinavian alphabet). Card shows the chosen ones (royal people). In Israel T tattoo was worn by royal people (czarist) on their foreheads. Tau cross – sign of chosen ones.

The Hanged's hands are tied behind and he can't change current situation though one leg is free. Person is forced to overlook his attitude towards life and life brings back him to the same goals and ideals that he turned away from. In the Wyatt's Tarot card deck the Hanged man is hanged up on his right foot while in the earlier, for example, Marseilles Tarot he is hanged up on his left foot and money is falling out of his pockets. It is related to the Judas' betrayal and betrayal generally. During the Middle ages thieves and traitors were hung up this way.

„Traitor" is another name of this card. He hangs and doesn't see any path or way out, is suspended in his own problems. The Hanged has bended one of his legs so that he could form the upside-down triangle. Legs form cross and head with hands from triangle (symbolizes growth and spirituality, rising). This shape forms upside-down sulfur sign and that means end of a huge work. Card turned upside down symbolizes loss of spiritual abilities. This card symbolizes transition from the higher to lower level or transition from conscious to unconscious state, which means sacrifice, refusal of one thing due to another. Square symbolizes everything what is material or has outer shape.

Noble meaning of this card is person's sacrifice for others.

Whole body, legs, triangle – reaching for one's ideals, striving to outer space or clouds, progress, development.

Triangle turned upside down is the sign of the Moon, also symbol of female origin denoting fertility, rain; symbolizes Great Mother 'Yin'. Card also has meanings of fear, death fears, fear of loneliness, time of having no purpose, obstacles. Process itself has to change to the direction of the changed attitude: find one's goals, defeat fears and realize its reasons. This is related with the "inner child". Process is long and demands to sacrifice what once was precious. That is why this card talks about sacrifice.

Triangle gives us an opportunity to grow, develop (meant by inner growth, not outer). Special rays of light indicate that person is discovering or has discovered the essence, right way out/solution, self-understanding, started to shine from the inside, found the light he was looking for. All cards from 12 to 21 denote path of liberation to fullness. Cards are going to show conversion of the triangle to the straight position, restoration of self-being and potential (up to 21 card). And spirituality becomes higher than matter.

Left leg, left side is responsible for intuition and is controlled by the right side. Being hung up on the left foot means that we have closed down our intuition, hang it up even without understanding it, unconsciously.

A person dangled in the material world, he has to glance back into oneself, come back to spirituality.

Face expression doesn't show any pain or suffering except deep thoughtfulness because this hard challenge was his own choice.

A living tree whose leaves symbolize living force, new opportunity became gallows. Rope is the connection with the outer space, wish to rise.

This card is the symbol of standing on one's head possessing meaning of different assessment of pecuniary system, peculiar renewal and revival.

This card can indicate fluctuation. Round the head of the Hanged there are 40 rays of light, which are human light, his wishes that he abandoned.

This card symbolizes inner middle age crisis of 25-45 year old person. Archetype: sacrifice.

The astrological point: Neptune (illusions).

Kabbalistic equivalent: letter arem.

Number 12 symbolizes 12 astrological signs; denotes spiritual and earthly order. Person is trying to discover oneself.

We have a lot of plans, actively participate in one or another sphere and after some time when relationship or business does not turn out as it was expected we begin to realize that our old goals mean nothing because our final destination didn't take us far. It is necessary to overlook our system of values what 12th arcana is. This card can also mean compulsion, forced actions, if comes together with bad cards such as Death, Devil, Moon or The Emperor (turned upside down) can have a meaning of violent death.

Meanings
Card position "straight"

General meaning: challenges, sacrifice, prudence, intuition, sagacity, isolation, prophecy, meditation, visualization, clairvoyant

Events: Hopeless situation, noose awaits, falling into the trap, going deep into events; alcoholism, drug addiction, arrest

Business and work: arrest, basic business, underground works, work in a shelf, production losses, output drop, stagnation, sticking in one's problems

Relationship: Inevitably status quo will be held out, drags one another, forced relationship, victim, reject unsatisfactory relationship, change something, sensual, dreamy, romantic, do not be afraid to be yourself

Health: Suffering, illness, psychics, light addiction, autism, depression, blood pressure, stroke , suffering from a spiritual either mental pain

Psychological characteristics: consciousness: penetration into the essence of things, new attitude, strong inner power, delicate person who is able to penetrate the essence of things

Advice: Change your attitude, arm oneself with patience

Warning: It's useless to hold on to the past; don't try to speed up events especially using force: it will get only worse; may other people's interests never be above or below yours.

Result: Going into the situation, necessity to live it down, you will have to abdicate something, you will flounder in the old problems

Card turned upside-down

General meaning: Incomprehension, reluctance to grow up. Pride, egoism, self-love, materialism. Crowd, clairvoyant, wants to remain as a child, reluctance to make decisions

Events: Alcohol and drug addiction (severe form), inability to control one's emotions

Business and work: Immaturity of attitudes, misunderstanding of the situation, shallow attitude, pity (person is very sorry for oneself) speculation (negative denial), carelessly do work

Relationship: Requirement of one's by any means, manipulation, despair; choice of any partner, the first person who comes across without paying attention to his character; instead of looking for ones path you will hold on to your former relationship; one night sex (king of scepters, henchman)

Health: Death either recovery

Psychological characteristics: conservatism and narrowness of thinking, shamefulness (excessive timidity, restriction), experience of hard times

Advice: Imagine you were in a position of beloved, love yourself very much

Warning: For the improvement of the situation self-love can be great obstacle, self-deception

Result: Perception, changes in life, liberation; it's not as bad as it seems: situation has to be looked over; ploys will work out according to destiny though result will let you down: you will be hoping for one but as a result get another.

The Hanged+The Fool – delayed childbirth
The Hanged+The Magician – difficulties in communicating with relatives
The Hanged+The High Priestess – inner crisis
The Hanged+The Empress – a way out from a difficult situation
The Hanged+The Emperor – dismissal from the capacity

The Hanged +The Hierophant – spiritual changes

The Hanged +Lovers – forced partnership, difficulties in taking some solutions

The Hanged +The Chariot – delayed trip

The Hanged +Strength – inner fight, increased pressure

The Hanged +Hermit – meditations, health problems of the elderly relative

The Hanged +Wheel of Fortune – positive changes of destiny, going out of the crisis

The Hanged +Justice – delay, document delay

The Hanged +Death – crisis

The Hanged +Sequence – compulsory restrictions, arrest

The Hanged +Devil– permanent drinking

The Hanged +Tower – detention, redundancy

The Hanged +Star – reorientation, goals review

The Hanged +Moon – alcohol usage

The Hanged +Sun – delayed childbirth

The Hanged +Judgment – liberation from a hard situation

The Hanged +World – exiting spiritual crisis, complete acquittal

13 card – DEATH

1 – The old name: scythe.

2-Archetype: divergence, death.

3 – The astrological point: Scorpio (movement) – traditional Zodiac sign identified with death.

4 – Kabbalistic equivalent:

Letter: Nun

Third karmic card.

Death – skeleton of a pawn or cavalier (can wear monk's clothes or armour). A scythe, bow with arrows or flag in the hand. Scythe or sickle reminds sickle of a moon and denotes symbol of all natural phenomena such as floods and low tides. Flag is the symbol of what disappears and reappears. Bow and arrows shoots through and boat transfers to another world.

Skeleton with armours denote emblem of the first-ever and greatest God because he is the body fundament. The Apocalypse cavaliers are thought to be oppression, hunger, war, death. Armours are the human's material shell. White horse is the symbol of purificated physical wishes.

Underneath, people of carious social and spiritual levels are lying (clergyman, king and a child); this is meant to say that everybody are subordinate to death.

A feather on the head – Maat the Goddess of justice. She was seen as an underworld goddess to whom Anubis escorted dead souls from the Wheel of Fortune. Maat would put good and bad deeds on a scale and decide where to send soul further. Feather was used as a lever. A horse is an animal that transmits or escorts soul to the Dead World.

White colour – renewal, purification.

Flag with five-leaves flower – white mystic rose which is symbol of new life and purification.

Dead takes all, taking away old and bringing new. One state changed by another, one end of the stage allows a new start for another.

Death is the exchange but not the river of death that tells world from the shadow kingdom apart. River symbolizes transition from one stage to another.

There is a boat by the bank used to reach the other world..

Sun between two towers is the door to another world, distinguishes earthly life from ethereal (dead) world. It is time when everything you lived for vanishes into non-existence and you can only observe and that will be the right position. Sun – birth, revival.

Meanings
Card position "straight"

General meaning: The end, mortality, destruction, recession, exhaustion

Events: divergence, beginning of something new, overhaul, purification from enchantment, loss of the source of the money

Business and work: Business closure, previous career crisis, labour quitting, great losses or trade break down, plastic surgery, dumps
Relationship: End of the break up with partner, category, renewed relationship

Health: Improvement after a crisis, ability to regenerate, enchantment, removal of bewitchment

Psychological characteristics: Consciousness: perception that nothing is eternal under the Sun, category, responsibility, prone to aggression, fear of death

Advice: Let go what is old, let it be finished so new could begin

Warning: Don't make any steps leading nowhere, don't be categorical, don't destroy everything around you, don't make any steps that have no perspectives

Result: exit, giving space for what is new, sometimes this card renders person who has connection with death and revival i.e.: restorer, surgeon, or priest conducting funeral ceremonies

Card turned upside-down

General meaning: inaction, inertia, dream, lethargy, stoniness, fear of changes

Events: Hope downfall, negative changes, disorder, unnecessary affairs

Business and work: bankruptcy proceedings, bankrupt, external controller, resuscitation, protracted crisis

Relationship: Long agony in a relationship, unnecessary affection, wrong attitude towards the leaving of a close person

Health: illness, low eneregtics, if illness has prolonged then improvement appears

Psychological characteristics: fears, resistance to changes, fear of responsibility, phobia

Advice: Endure the situation, wait for the right time, ignore
Warning: Don't stretch rubber, don't cut slice by slice
Result: Situation isn't finished, situation will never finish

Death+The Fool – tattoo, piercing
Death+The High Priestess – wedding, lovers
Death+The Empress – child abandoning home
Death+The Emperor – transition to a new position
Death+The Hierophant – the elderly family member is having a crisis
Death+Lovers – divorce, divergence
Death+The Chariot – car breakdown or maintenance
Death+Strength – injuries
Death+Hermit – end of loneliness
Death+Wheel of Fortune – end of lucky period
Death+Justice – a defeat in a Judgement
Death+the Hanged – crisis
Death+Devil – crisis
Death+Tower – mass redundancies, injury
Death+Star – apartment reppairs

Death+Moon – emotional crisis
Death+Sun – Caesarean section, plastic surgery
Death+Judgement – solution to a critical situation
Death+World – health crisis, unrealized journey

14 card – TEMPERANCE

1 – The old name: genius of sun and two Hindu.
2-Archetype: the golden mean, harmony.
3 – The astrological point: Sagittarius (anger) and Virgo.
4 – Kabbalistic equivalent:
Letter: Samekh

Card depicts angel with wings and two goblets in his hands and he uses them to pour water from one goblet to another. Card symbolizes unity of contrasts. Water symbolizes constant stream of vital force and circulation. As if pours, as if mixes. One goblet has the live energy of Yang and the other – dead water, Yin, the female energy. Same meaning possesses angel's figure depicting one leg wade into the water and the other is on the ground. This way the figure is like a bridge connecting two contrasts. Earth – material world and consciousness. The integration process of inner and outer forces, mental strength recovery of male and female. Process of the Hanged's reverse.

Gobles are golden and silver. That is sun and the moon. Sun is the male origin and moon is the symbol of female origin. Water pouring is the eternal circulation, eternal circulation of energy in the universe.

One goblet symbolizes past and the other future. The rainbow stream between them denotes present people who don't understand presence at all. Everything repeats (even situations repeat). Flowing water means movement, it is the circulation of the energy, feelings. Wings behind the angel are visible. This figure symbolizes the archangel Michael who is the angel of time (like god he is the angel of fire and south).

White clothes, golden triangle in the square – material world, as a symbol square is the sign of saint book Torah and between human and God – symbol of universe. Spirit imprisoned in the substance (triangle in the square).

God symbolizes the trinity, world of the ideas. Dot in the middle of disc in the forehead is the human soul. Flowers symbolize goddess Isis – goddess of the rainbow and Sagittarius (the astrological sign).

Long way is the way of moderation which is one of the 4 most important virtues. According to Aristotle feeling of moderation is the most important for the human being. Crown shows that person has found his path, self I, new goals that are closely related to his spirit, soul; and everything is a one long way to reach it. Watching through the time perspective, this card is very long means process will take from 1.5 to 3 years. Person will take a particular way and won't have any possibilities to turn to another. This card denotes renewal of spiritual and physical forces, reconciliation and adaption to the new situation. Person feels balance in his life, stability as well. This arcana has the meaning of strength of consciousness and ability to withstand to any environmental impact.

Self-control dominates, time comprehension, essence of the circulation of everything in the world. Moderation card is the last card of the second seven; it is the card of middle correction.

Cards of the first seven are the cards belonging to outer development. They denote the end of one life and rapid beginning of the second life that is embodied by the cards of the second seven.

Meanings
Card position "straight""

General meaning: thrift, retention, management; tranquility, suitable moderation, peace, stability, accommodation , renewal of spiritual and physical strength

Events: Long events, constrained actions, imprisonment, restrictions, persistence, experience accumulation

Business and work: with the sword's 7 – tranquiller life), art, beauty industry, homeopathy, pharmacology, watch industry, perfumery, computer production

Relationship: constant, long lasting, slowly developing, without any passion, casual,   according to the rules; love devoted to oneself and others, love and commitment, love will bring peace and tranquility.

Health: Limited mobility, slow process; good health either slow recovery, recovery

Psychological characteristics: consciousness: coherent thinking, searching for the golden mean, slow person, perceptive, tranquiller, punctual, he helps to solve the conflicts

Advice: To find the golden mean, try to find various experience, wait out

Warning: Don't waist time, don't go in to useless work; don't do anything carelessly, Do not engage in the pleasures of the moment

Result: peace, recovery, choice of the right moment, affair will drag on

Card turned upside-down

General meaning: Determined however wrong act, two deeds simultaneously, wrong attitude towards life and people

Events: Unreasonable behavior, breach of rules, escape, attempt to speed up events; inconsistency, laziness

Business and work: Breach of terms, defects, business growth range, too big thrift, local network, computer viruses, excessive punctuality

Relationship: desire to revitalize the relationship, total stagnation, weakening over the years; extremist; competition of some interests, shallow

Health: Healthy and active person, fever, sleep disorders, unconventional mode

Psychological characteristics: variable, hesitant

Advice: refrain from sudden and reckless behaviors

Warning: Impatient and irritable person will create confusion around him

Result: Wrong timing, relationship without any changes, everything will happen faster then expected

Temperance+The Fool – prolonged journey
Temperance+The Magician – permanent education
Temperance+The High Priestess – practicing of alternative medicine
Temperance+The Empress – accommodation purchase
Temperance+The Emperor – permanent position
Temperance+ The Hierophant – thesis preparation
Temperance+Lovers – love triangle, long lasting events
Temperance+The Chariot – long lasting journey
Temperance+Strength – limited abilities
Temperance+Hermit – permanent solitude
Temperance+Wheel of Fortune – speeding up of events, long waited luck
Temperance+Justice – long process
Temperance+the Hanged – prolonged situation
Temperance+Death – stopping of a long process
Temperance+Devil – bank credits
Temperance+ Tower – acquisition of a real estate
Temperance+Star – permanent plans, perspective job
Temperance+Moon – cruise
Temperance +Sun – fortunate career
Temperance+Judgement – escape out of frames
Temperance+World – emigration, accommodation receipt

15 card–DEVIL

1-The old name: Typhon.

2-Archetype: the dark side, seductions, evil, sin.

3 – The astrological point: Capricon (mirth, laugh). Create, no matter what people say.

4 – Kabbalistic equivalent:

Letter: Ayin

Devil denotes various obstacles and if we get free from them then we would get vitality and energy. Devil is depicted as half human and half goat, huge with a tail, bat's wings and small horns. It is the evil force or dark side of a human. He is sitting on one side of the cube.

Upside-down pentagram is the sign of evil, upside-down place of a person in the world. Goat of Mendes muzzle fits into the upside-down pentagram. Goat symbolizes voluptuousness, abuse of the animal instincts. Horns symbolize sexuality. His pose mocks gesture of a priest. Mercury sign is in the middle of the abdomen, in the other hand sign of the Saturn. Saturn symbolizes stability. Black colour denotes earth, instead of scepter he has a torch which deceptive light will lead people to their collapse but at the same time it can be light.

Bat's wings are the attribute of dark creature which means that it is necessary to shake off superstition fear.

He is akin to Greek god Pan. He was god of indomitable sexuality and lust. He symbolizes out natural demands.

Naked male and female confined to cube is the image of frailty. Chain is captivity and addiction to the sensual desires. This is the pose before the sin; their love became downfall but not the lift. In this card their love faded away and became earthly, that love inflamed disagreements and chained to the material world. Devil is the contortion of the reality, human's origin as an animal, addiction.

This card is the period of challenges (desire of a material wealth, mysterious passion, striving for a comfort), if a person extracts this card means he has confronted his attributes face to face, ones that dropped off the chain. Person has to try to realize their cause.

Card denotes desire of material and physical goods, sometimes it shows that person is prisoner of his own feelings (sensuality, ambition of power, addictions)

Capricon the Satan. Satan shows the dark side: for The Magician it is black magic, for The High Priestess it is part of her negative archetype, The Hierophant – shaming to be saint, naïve, for Lovers – fight for authority or degenerated relationship which became depended on sex without love, Justice- corruption either inability to admit its untruth, mistakes. This card shows that we are playing with fire and ought to be more mindful.

Person becomes such as world is, which forces man to fight for existence. 15th arcana is the dark side of all arcanas, all matters, all Zodiac signs. Evil is not only as the compound part of human's existence but also life's in general. Human being has to converge into dialogue with the Satan. You take for granted matters that cannot be right. Satan can signify desire of material or physical wealth also controls others. Sometimes denotes displeased erotic lust.

This card in a psychological manner of speaking is something that can scare us, our encounter with the inner I that is in the back of our minds. In our subconsciousness there are particular features, thoughts and wishes which we consciously do not acknowledge, do not wish to and are ashamed of.

Those desires, stresses, experience are very strong and since they have not been gone through, consciousness pushes them away to subconsciousness, however they do not disappear. Precisely this human's part in the religion was called Satan, satanic desires; this is associated with the subconsciousness. What was forbidden was thought to be from Satan but not from God. What we do not acknowledge however keep inside us, forms our life and later we wonder why one or another event has happened. And if we have strong energy, which is closed, this energy will live in us and those little Satans will test us, form our lives. Whole life experience is restoration of plenitude which means to restore those emotions that we ousted.

Meanings
Card position "straight"

General meaning: power, perish, special efforts, cruelty, blindness, weakness, materiality, destiny

Events: Huge arrears, addiction, attraction, criminal case, illegal actions, treachery

Business and work: Dependency in some matters, dirty money, money laundering, criminal business; systemic management, apparent employment, production harmful for health, waste, environmental pollution, career illnesses

Relationship: emotional, material, sexual dependency; voluptuousness, curvature, passions

Health: High temperature, consequences of bad habits; sepsis, surfeit

Psychological characteristics: Consciousness: encountering with own shadow; advisor who has a great life experience, it can show black extrasensory or person who works with negative energy

Advice: Do not become addictive, do not lend or borrow, don't entangle in doubtful commitment

Warning: Fear of temptations, see a doctor, avoid easy money or paths, do not judge things only by their exterior

Result: authority, manipulation of others; coercion, efforts, force, destiny, catastrophe

Card turned upside-down

General meaning: recovery, brainstorm, liberation; liberation from anxiety

Events: Addiction to bad habits, debauchery, attempt to free from particular addiction, oppression

Business and work: Liberation from addiction, debt, affection, criminal case, total downfall (together with a bad card)

Relationship: Liberation from dependency, recusancy, sexual curvature, coercion, pornography

Health: Weakened health, rash, organism after illness, loss of strength

Psychological characteristics: pettiness, blindness, cynic, improvidence, you might have felt spark of God's blessedness

Advice: Do not abuse authority; don't manipulate people
Warning: Do not manipulate people; overcoming low incentives, leaving the shadow
Result: Evil fate, weakness; conquest of fears, you are not controlling events, events are controlling you

Devil+the Hanged – alcohol abuse
Devil +Death – crisis
Devil+Temperance – bank credits
Devil+Tower – bank loans, bewitchment, theft
Devil+Star – computer breakdown
Devil+Moon – alcohol abuse
Devil+Sun – great profit
Devil+Judgement – receipt of a bit amount of money, liberation from addiction
Devil +World – temptation, journey abroad

16 card – TOWER

THE TOWER.

1 –The old name: razed tower (shelter), war.
2-Archetype: destruction, earthquake, catastrophe..
3 – the astrological point: Mars (god of war). Planet – Uranium.
4 – Kabbalistic equivalent:
Letter: Pei

If we are keen to build new structure then it is necessary to demolish the old one. New conducting methods are required because old ones became too restrictive. Events rise not from the person's will but due to the circumstances. Victim of the circumstances.
Tower is sending a message that formed convenient situation should be challenged. Tower is a sign of imprisonment and limitation. It is the symbol of male origin, explosion – movement, it is forced collapse of the old orthodTaurus, lightning – divine perception that can see through and destroy the old order. Lightning is God's sign, the finger of God. It is new visions and opportunities that have to be pointed out. Crown is the symbol of authority, aspiration for authority, autocracy, our illusions. Falling crown – collapse of the illusion. Clouds (black colour is the colour of the terra) are gleam, light. Twinkles (from one side 10 and from another 12) coming out from the lightning (12 Zodiac signs) is the positive energy that comes after downfall. These twinkles symbolizes positive creative energy which comes out of destruction. 2 figures are falling from the tower are the symbol of the material force

breakthrough. Those forces can deal with anybody and at the same time it is the emblem of competition that has a bad ending. 2 people symbolize meditation, also can depict brainwave.

Card shows that in the nearest future irreversible and unpleasant changes will occur. It is important to be able to look during the event of danger straight into it's the eye.

There is no need to restore ruins, novelty has to be created. Very rapid and sudden end of a situation. It is conflict, fall, end of existing living order, great losses (together with bad cards), time of "good strip" is coming to an end (together with good cards).

Structure in our life which has become obsolete. This arcana is linked with mother: child has to withdraw from his mother because being with her is already an obstacle for his development. Present system of values will bother him and the tower will go negatively. Creation of inner limitations, values, tower symbolizes inner system of values which crux is egoism and desire to be higher then everybody else. Such system of values sooner or later will be destroyed. Everything falls down by Judgments of lightning – interference of some higher force, pure, positive energy which dismantles, destroys those qualities and values. We all have a potential and if we do not realize it, available energy is nowhere disused; a situation will come up which will demolish that system and person will be forced to develop and improve. This card talks about brainstorm – discovery of aims, ambitions (we discover them ourselves or we are forced to move on).

This card is especially strong energetically.

Meanings
Card position "straight"

General meaning: Disappointment, resentfulness, fraud, coming apart, destruction, imprisonment, collapse, accident

Events: „explosion of a bomb", accident, redundancy, scandal; bankruptcy (conceptive as well), liberation

Business and work: force major (insuperable force), downfall, accident, failed expectations and plans, redundancy, loss of position, impeachment, construction business

Relationship: furious, bitter, cruel, hierarchical, strong sexual attraction

Health: shock, heart attack, a swipe, loss of consciousness, decline of personality

Psychological characteristics: Consciousness: fail of an idea of great importance, sudden brainstorm

Advice: Take all possible precautions, don't be a dreamer, go down to the ground, don't lose your head
Warning: Dangerous time awaits, hairpin, blow on health; you are lost, avoid unjustifiable risk
Result: Eruption to the freedom
Card turned upside-down
General meaning: Mental recession, downfall of illusions and dramatic changes; crisis can be adjusted

Events: Secret agreement, illegal construction, natural phenomena caused artificially, assassination; imprisonment; natural disasters

Business and work: Destruction of a competitor,mental recession, accident with happy ending
Relationship: Weakening of sexual attraction, reconciliation in a much lower level, after stormy discussions

Health: madness, fake patient, rapid overcoming of an illness, death from an accident, neurosis

Psychological characteristics: Fear of downfall, syndrome of unhappy childhood, completely alone

Advice: Break away from own or others egoism and ignorance traps
Warning: Do not fear of misfortune, don't attach to the result
Result: nsufficient preparation to conquer obstacle, expectancy of appreciation for well done work

Tower +Fool – minor troubles, injured child
Tower +The Magician – fights with relatives, divorce, hospital treatment
Tower + The High Priestess – energetic decline
Tower +The Empress – divergence, acquisition of an apartment
Tower +The Emperor – clerk of a high rank
Tower +The Hierophants – divorce, educational institution
Tower +Lovers – sudden divergence
Tower +The Chariot – accident
Tower +Strength – illness
Tower + Hermit – obtainment of insurance rebate, elderly person's illness
Tower + Wheel of Fortune – natural disasters

Tower +Justice – arrest, Judgement hearing, divorce

Tower + the Hanged – arrest, involuntary termination of employment

Tower +Death – car accident, illness

Tower +Devil – credit

Tower +Star – liberation from the limitations

Tower +Moon – troubles in the water

Tower +Sun – perspective idea

Tower +Judgment – acquitted sentence, extrication, release from prison

Tower +World – acquisition of an apartment

17 card – STAR

THE STAR.

1 – The old name: the star of Magi.

2-Archetype: alive water, hope.

3 — The astrological point: Aquarius (meditation and idea). Planet Saturn, Uranium.

4 – Kabbalistic equivalent:

Letter: Tzadei.

. It is the light that brightens the darkness. Naked woman is the symbol of truth, purity, pure intentions. There are two pitchers in the hands. Water is being spilled on the ground and into the cluster. Terra is the symbol of growth of matter and cluster is accumulation of spiritual subconsciousness. She is pouring water which is born in the outer space. Water has the power of purging. Water does never drain without purpose – what is given away comes back. Water symbolizes purging energy and it is our subconsciousness as well.

Water which is flowing in a stream on a ground symbolizes material growth, yang energy. And water which is flowing in to the cluster symbolizes female yin energy, spiritual growth. Card depicts unification of two origins - male and female. After the destruction made by the Tower which had destroyed everything, as a result only purity and everything what is clean in person was left.

It is the symbol of hope, revival, great success at any work. 1 big and 7 little start: 1 big – center, 7 chakras (7 stars). Star is a hope, ideals and intelligence from the alien world; it is the first arcana that is related with cosmos, The Magician's star that symbolizes elements of planets and others' natural forces unity. 7 stars compose a sickle with handle which is the symbol of Saturn (lord or the water who talks about longevity). Stars symbolize help from the outer space either universe.

A star directs right path in the dark, 7 stars surrounds that bigger one and compose the 8th star which symbolizes revival and baptism.

8 is the symbol of the middle of the path which goes from earthly to spiritual side.

Big star is the concentration over the great aim. Star sticks out with its size, brightness, has 8 beams. It is the star of wisdom. The Magicians' symbol. Star symbolizes secrets of destiny closed under seven locks, wish to live and optimism. Advice: protect hope.

Around the woman there is a beautiful nature, peace, far away in a tree a songbird. Ibis is the bird particularly associated with the god Thoth and is symbol of soul's ability to rise into a higher plane.

Astrologers' card – star. Astrology is mother of all arts. Hope has to be conscious. Person has to do whatever he can and let go the situation. Good influence over others, vital energy, trust in ones powers, optimistic approach to life.

Card shows that person has just started to create his karma; ideas coming into his mind are very correct, pure and are supported by the outer space. Acts taken by the person will give fruits for several years and the result will be after some years (5-6 years approximately). Card depicts the right tongue language.

Meanings
Card position "straight"

General meaning: hope, great perspective, loss, need, future, assurance on the day of tomorrow, talents

Events: Long preparation, necessary procedures, strict order and Temperance of neutral events, discovery of a new attitude towards things

Business and work: fortune, perspective activity, computer equipment, software supply, dietology, Alternative Medicine, job with a long-term perspective

Relationship Blissful future with the bright future; comprehend, spiritual, delicate, extol, new friend, no sexual relationship

Health: : Renewed body, second breath, recovery after a tough illness, good physical health, may be depression

Psychological characteristics: Consciousness: view extension, new perspectives, knows how to make good use of freedom of choice, inner liberty

Advice: Believe in your luck and future; reach for high aims, be open to innovations
Warning: Don't live in dreams about future, so you wouldn't lose today's chance; don't bring together the ends of everything to the bodily origin
Result: Trust in outer space, inspiring goal
Card turned upside-down
General meaning: doubts, absence of perspective, failure; downfall of hopes and talents;

Events: unclear procedures, poor and lifeless feasts, full of pathos official style, „brainwash"

Business and work: failure, impossible plans, program closure, the absence of data, exhaustion
Relationship: Mercantil, practical, utilitarian; unethical behavior, pride, insincere, deceptive

Health: Long-drawn-out treatment, hysteria, hopeless condition, an incurable chronic disease

Psychological characteristics: Bad self-assessment, feelings blockade, mask, fear of being oneself

Advice: Ask for a wise advice, leave empty hopes, be more practical
Warning: Difficult times are coming up; downfall of hopes
Result: Loss of self-confidence

Star+ Fool – child's initiation
Star+The Magician – right actions
Star+The High Priestess – creative inspiration
Star+The Empress – visits to a cosmetologist or beauty salon
Star+The Emperor – new perspective position, meeting with partner
Star+The Hierophant – high recognition
Star+Lovers – new love
Star+The Chariot – right direction, trendy car

Star+Strength– organism purification
Star+Hermit – meditations
Star+ Justice – perspective contract
Star+ the Hanged – living in a dream
Star+Death – plastic surgery
Star+Devil – sexual attraction, high level of creative skills
Star+ Tower – disastrous dreams
Star+Moon – fear of realization of a plan
Star+Sun – child birth
Star+Judgement – realization of a dream
Star+World – moving out/migration

18 card – MOON

1 – The old name: twilight.

2-Archetype: night, kingdom of darkness.

3 – The astrological point: Pisces (dream). Planet Moon. Sun in the 7th house.

4 – Kabbalistic equivalent:

Letter: Kaf.

The main feature of this card is lack of clarity. Huge moon illuminates ground and river. Moon is guardian of subconsciousness, state of mind. It is related to water, the female origin, emotions and intuition. Moon is the sun of the other world and is related with magic. The moon goddess Selene was an enchantress, protector of witches. She was the reason why Greeks read all the spells during the full moon.

In the card the moon is depicted in the 3rd phase, which symbolizes three stages of woman's life: girl-old woman.

Ancient nations imagined moon as a womb and new life coming out of it. This card forecasts variable period of life. It is wrong time for serious decisions because this card is quite on edge. However there is some creativity in this card. We see the moon and it is night rendering danger and fears. The water cluster at night symbolizes fears and misgiving. Water is an element from which everything appeared, it is world's evolution.

A Coming out on a dry land Cancer – symbol of going out of the sea bowel, world's evolution (human's way to surface out of the water). Evolution of psychological development connected with subconsciousness and way out of deep subconsciousness into the consciousness.

Armours – material covering, mystery, feeling of safety.

A water cluster is a symbol of subconsciousness and human's as well, who is searching for reality, symbol, illusions.

Cancer is a symbol of a creation that is afraid to go forward so he is moving backwards to the darkness.

A path that is winding between 2 towers is the symbol of path leading to the ignorance.

Towers are thought to be towers of consciousness and subconsciousness. They divide material world from the world of illusions; they are gates of heaven and hell and this way instinctive half of subconsciousness appears. *Wolf is still not tamed to human but the dog is; this shows the ability to tame and use natural force and force of subconsciousness. This card also talks about very slow changes because a cancer that is moving towards and backwards is depicted.*

A dog and a wolf are howling at the moon. Dog and wolf symbolize fears born of our mind, animal's instincts. Wolf – nature before human's appearance and symbolizes killer, werewolf, enemy. Dog is a tamed wolf and symbolizes friend, loyalty.

Crags – world of minerals.

Grass and flowers – world of vegetation.

This card doesn't denote compulsorily person.

This card is symbol of illusions, dreams, creativity. It ends cycle of Zodiac signs. Card appeared on the line of Pisces and Aries where the astrological wheel ends and starts again; and it is believed that there is a grey vague zone which is dangerous because path becomes invisible.

In ancient times this card was called twilight because the cycle goes to an end and the new one doesn't begin because it was thought that a person had gone too far so he could turn around. That vague zone is dangerous. One of the meanings of a card is that someone wants to mislead you, someone is telling tales and people believe in him, person doesn't really understand what is going on around him because he is living in his own illusions and is hiding his head in the ground like an ostrich.

This card warns that a person has to act carefully; impudent behavior with the obscurity is the same as making martyr of oneself. Observe, listen and be quiet.

Card of subconsciousness. This card is the last phase of getting deep into oneself. After it everything will be fine. This card is being compared to the day period before the dawn, the most dark time of a night, after which dawn comes.

Meanings
Card position "straight"

General meaning: Secret enemies, danger, darkness, deception, gossips, occult forces, fickleness, prophetic dreams, fear

Events: Irreversible losses, fermentation, congestion, deception, treachery

Business and work: Occult business, night works, risky operations, dangerous career categories, huge monetary flow, contraband, illegal tourism

Relationship: Disappointment, expectancy, insincerity, duality, hypocrisy, solitude

Health: Procedures of purging are necessary, tissue density (tumor), precipitate on the partition of an intestine, fears, drug addiction

Psychological characteristics: Consciousness: growth of the forces of subconsciousness, *inner anxiety, carefulness, reticence, apparent lack of confidence*

Advice: Don't be afraid, follow in someone's footsteps, don't lie, reduce wave but stay on the flow, don't diverge from a collective, guard trade secrets

Warning: Don't stay alone with difficulties, don't shrink into oneself, you are being cheated, don't wander in the dark, don't go into world of illusions and hallucinations

Result: Deepness of self perception, gossips, mistakes

Card turned upside-down

General meaning: Illusions, hallucinations, disappointment; an end to disgrace, instability

Events: Secret complicates events, hidden processes

Business and work: Illegal business categories, regression in the ploy, crowd, influence on a strapping business, small cog in a big company

Relationship: Total reticence and illegality, opacity, sincere love and concern, misapprehension and difficulties in a relationship with mother

Health: Sanity illnesses, manias, exaggerated enthusiasm, fear of people, obtrusive state, menstruate cycle disorders

Psychological characteristics: Enlarged sensitivity

Advice: Dream and create

Warning: Disinclination to go forwards, you don't solve problems that have to be solved

Result: deception, mistakes in trivialities

Moon+Fool – trip to the seaside
Moon+The Magician – deception of a close person, no self-confidence
Moon+The High Priestess – immersion in oneself
Moon+The Empress – gossip
Moon+The Emperor – management fraud
Moon+The Hierophant – communication with mother
Moon+Lovers – secret meetings
Moon+The Chariot – trip to the seaside
Moon+Strength – water resource
Moon+Hermit– lonely woman, document falsification
Moon+Wheel of Fortune – flood, repetitive situation from the past
Moon+Justice – document falsification
Moon+ the Hanged – alcohol abuse
Moon +Death – emotional crisis
Moon+Sequency– emotional harmony
Moon+Devil – fraud, emotional and alcohol addiction
Moon+Tower – swindle, flood
Moon+Star – victory against doubts
Moon+Sun – emotional rise
Moon+Judgement – meeting with mother or grandmother
Moon+World – voyage

19 card – SUN

THE SUN .

1 – The old name: bright light.
2-Archetype: day, kingdom of light.
3 – the astrological point: Sun (god of pleasures and riches).
4 – Kabbalistic equivalent:
Letter: Reish

A Sun with human's face is the symbol of all Gods (Jesus Christ, Buddha, Apollo). It is the vital power, origin of the outer space and personality's basis. Sun is the male origin, energy of movement, action. Direct beams – consciousness, yang energy, active, wavy – subconsciousness, yin, passive energy: those beams warm sunflowers and these two energies give growth, energy of action and energy of keeping. A child is sitting on a horse is symbol of immortality, resurrection; child symbolizes beginning of something new, growth of inner and outer forces, birth of something new. Naked child – intentions, purity of the heart. Horse is the energy of the sun controlled by the vital force. Horse's white colour is colour of destiny, luck. White horse is also symbol of mastering ones destiny, great forces of life. Flag and wreath are symbols of victory, freedom. Wall is either protection or obstacles. Wall protects person from others glances. Wall denotes growth of opportunities though there will be some obstacles and for a child to go trough a wall energy usage is required. This energy is symbolized through a red flag; child will have to use doggedness.

Sunflower is the expression of sun energy on the ground, growth. It is the symbol of sun or symbol of a newborn soul. Red colour – energy of planet Mars and energy of action.

Card shows that sun is the light perspective and positive attitude.

Day is the male origin – consciousness, mind. Mind has to be used with a great responsibility. Sun denotes wish fulfillment.

Card shows that events will take whole year duration.

Meanings
Card position "straight"

General meaning: Material wealth, fortunate (happy) marriage, vitality, satisfaction, warmth

Events: luck, clearing up, open actions, the emergence of new opportunities, influx of energy

Business and work: Abound in the market, gold rush, alcohol business, festivities, prestige relaxation, horse trade

Relationship: Kindness, warmth, reconciliation, forgiveness, frankness, self-sufficiency, trust, wish to show oneself and though it is empty however it is attracting attention

Health: Sun burn, sunstroke, energy, strong health, female alcoholism

Psychological characteristics: Consciousness: reveal of the Real I, *person who no matter what will reach his goal, individuality*

Advice: Try to set to work with optimism and joy to life

Warning: Don't overestimate your power, don't be naive, commonplace or carefree, don't get sun burned „giddiness with achievements", greediness

Result: Liberation from the dark / darkness defeat; full realization of personality, total safety

Card turned upside-down

General meaning: boastfulness, egoism, innocence; defeat, emptiness

Events: False announcement about the luck, achievement of misleading aims, inappropriate actions

Business and work: Empty appearance, alcoholism, exaggerated diligence, boastfulness, return to childhood, sacredness

Relationship: Cannot independently deal with problems, unfortunate marriage or love bond, party, empty, without any idea, boastfulness

Health: laziness, apathy, alcoholism

Psychological characteristics: Fear to act and loss

Advice: Ask for help
Warning: All who will try to change situation to the better will be disturbed by your cowardliness, pessimism and mind narrowness
Result: Marginal material wealth

Sun+ The Fool– bright appearance, child birth
Sun+The Magician – talent recognition
Sun+The High Priestess – jewelry purchase
Sun+The Empress – child birth, opening of a beauty salon
Sun+The Emperor – high rank obtainment
Sun+The Hierophant – popularity
Sun+ Lovers – love confession
Sun+The Chariot – bright career, prestige car
Sun+Strength – bright victory
Sun+Hermit – known specialist
Sun+Wheel of Fortune – huge success
Sun+Justice – victory in the Judgement
Sun+the Hanged – three day long alcohol abuse
Sun+Death – plastic surgery
Sun+ Temperance– equitable actions
Sun+Devil – big money
Sun+Tower – blow on the head
Sun+Star – fortunate actions
Sun+Moon– fight between mind and feelings
Sun+Judgement – child birth
Sun+World – worldwide known person

20 card – JUDGEMENT

1 – The old name: revival of the dead ones.

2-Archetype: rising from the dust Phoenix, treasure discovery, liberation, magical kiss.

3 – The astrological point: element of fire (that burns all obstacles). Planet Pluto (god of the inner fire). Jupiter/uranium harmonizes with the sun.

5 – Kabbalistic equivalent:

Letter: Shin

4 karmic card.

An angel is inviting all dead to rise. Bodies with the stretched out hands are rising out of the coffins, throw off shrouds, prepare for a new life that angel is suggesting.

It is reincarnation, resurrection after death. It is believed that all will rise to stand in from of the Last Judgment.

Revival – repetition. Angel is God's messenger who transmits important information. It is Archangel Gabriel – embodiment of the Lord's force – declaring the Last Judgment's day. Rising from the dead is the sign of changes denoting end of the world, transition from the earhly world to the future. Trumpet is connecting heaven and earth; symbolizes declaring of an important message. A flag with a cross is the symbol of Apocalypse according to Saint John. It is magic square of Mars.

3 shapes: male – consciousness, female – subconsciousness, child– spirit.

This is a human manifestation to the heavenly Trinity.

Female – L, child – U, male – X, LUX – light (pose of a letter). It is justification of ones actions.

The time has come to turn back and analyze, assume oneself and self-being. Self-analysis is necessary. It is time to manage all ploys and prepare for a new beginning. It is family card. In the puzzle it means that person has a family.

Meanings
Card position "straight"

General meaning: Change of a situation, renewal, way out (out of situation), solution, resurrection, revival

Events: judgment, final decision, salvation, lucky end, start everything from the beginning

Business and work: Revival of the former business, property issues, family business, treasure discovery, fact disclosure, renovation, museums, historic memorials, recovery, jewelry

Relationship: Real union (in every sense), forgiveness, relative, close, fraternal; or divergence, loss of a relationship

Health: Helpful medicine, remission, recovery, good heredity

Psychological characteristics: Consciousness: puberty, comprehension, freedom, strain to hold on to own emotions and avert to the past

Advice: Believe that solution of a problem is near; ask relatives for help

Warning: Don't forget relatives, family members; your roots are struck down

Result: Liberation from the previous destiny (karma)

Card turned upside-down

General meaning: Self-deception, self-limiting

Events: Refusal to take advantage of ones authority while solving serious problem; repetition of the past mistakes

Business and work: Useless efforts, tough family bond, treachery of a close one, absence of perspectives

Relationship: Inability to give freedom or relent; apparent reconciliation; hit own so others would fear; familiarity, imposed friendship

Health: Incurable disease, medicine helps however doesn't cure, slow recovery, bad heredity

Psychological characteristics: Fear of changes, pusillanimity, simplicity

Advice: It's time to change
Warning: Leaving mellowed changes aside, which conscience's voice is requiring, you are putting oneself into a stagnant swamp
Result: Decision, sentence

Judgement +The Fool – discovery of minor values, birthday
Judgement +Magician – return of a close person
Judgement +The High Priestess – revival of love
Judgement +The Empress – marriage
Judgement +The Emperor – restoration to office
Judgement +The Hierophant – family council
Judgement +Lovers – marriage
Judgement +The Chariot – relative advent
Judgement +Strength – recovery
Judgement +Hermit – divergence
Judgement +Wheel of Fortune – destiny change to the better
Judgement + Justice – property division, receipt of inheritance
Judgement +the Hanged – suspended sentence
Judgement +Death – crisis
Judgement +Devil – great values
Judgement +Tower – divergence, property division
Judgement +Star – revival of a dream, revealed talents
Judgement +Moon – jewelry theft
Judgement +Sun – child birth or birthday
Judgement +World – great inheritance

21 card – WORLD

THE WORLD.

1 – The old name: The Magicians' crown, The Magicians' wreath, Cosmos.

2-Archetype: the coronation of a hero, run to earth paradise.

3 – The astrological point: Saturn (prohibition, god of night and underworld)

4 – Kabbalistic equivalent: leter Tau

This arcana in the greek tradition matches name of cosmos and means peace, compatibility. Cosmos is born from chaos and after the apocalypse it becomes chaos again so that cosmos could reborn.

In the middle of the laurel wreath there is a dancing figure. Laurel is the sign of luck and great achievements. The oval is eternal revival (something ends and simultaneously something begins).

That oval at the same time is a wreath, symbol of the compatibility of the body and spirit, symbol of recognition and femininity.

Naked man – purity of the nature, beauty. Pose is the same as the Hanged man's but stagnation changes with the movement. Figure is dancing.

In the corners of the card we can see the same figures as in the Wheel of Fortune – those figures are 4 aspects of plentitude, it is astrological signs of Taurus, Lion, Scorpio, Eagle and Human.

Zodiac signs

Seasons

4 elements

5th element is denoted by the middle figure of alchemy. This figure is covered with cloth that is hermaphrodite; It symbolizes completeness and symbol of balance. In the hands of Androgen there are 2 scepters which denote wishes that came true.

This figure is holding 2 scepters that is 2 wills.

It is ability to join two contraries. Figure is holding scepters in one level and that means compatibility of all life forms. This man is dancing. Dance is union of all elements. Dynamic world. The man is created in order to enjoy life.

The symbols of Saturn are a purple scarf and pose.

This card symbolizes completeness. Everything what you've been up to is giving fruits. Well-earned relax, work is done and soon will come time to plan new deeds.

It is said that after achieving any goals a feeling of emptiness may appear and in this case a dancing figure becomes progeny in the womb, waiting for a revival as a The Fool. There is nothing more to learn, the end wreathes everything.

Meanings
Card position "straight"

General meaning: Guaranteed luck, extra compensation, place interchange, inertia, constancy, harmony

Events: Happy end, end of a journey, management of the customs procedures, trip to abroad, pomp, degree conferment, triumph

Business and work: Acquisition of a recognition, discovery of own purpose, end of work, finishing project, handling in object, thesis defense

Relationship: pride, conceit, divergence (75-85 %), joy, harmony; strong union (25%), agreement, bliss; sexual relationship with amount of partners, divorce

Health: pregnancy, virginity loss, ambiguous feeling, venereal disease

Psychological characteristics: Consciousness: reaching of a total comprehension, peace, patience, endurance

Advice: Don't be conceit, be simpler, don't enforce own advices

Warning: You are too conceit; after reaching goal don't lay on laurel, concentrate

Result: Restoration of former integrity; emigration; new level of consciousness, bliss in love and friendship

Card turned upside-down

General meaning: immovability, disappearance of a determination to fight

Events: Drowning of a new built ship, lowered into the water, too risky step, retirement, death

Business and work: Wrong steps, loss of interest in an activity, apparent reconciliation

Relationship: conceit, ignorance, denial, leaving to all four sides

Health: Uterus illnesses, overseas disease

Psychological characteristics: laziness, determination, egoism; inability to accept oneself as one is

Advice: Overcome inner obstacles

Warning: You are not taking last step

Result: Partial victory; end of spiritual work denoted to understand world and oneself

World +The Fool – child's trip abroad
World +The Magician – presentation
World +The High Priestess – secret information
World +The Empress– new relationship
World +The Emperor – international character
World +The Hierophant – worldwide recognition
World +Lovers – number of love romances
World +The Chariot – trip abroad
World +Strength – rally
World +Hermit – retirement
World +Wheel of Fortune – change of residence
World + Justice – peaceful settlement of disputes
World + the Hanged – forced deferment of a trip
World +Death – crisis
World +Sequence – end of a long term project
World + Devil –sex meetings
World +Tower– foreign subsidiary

World +Star – aircraft construction
World +Moon – resort by the sea, infidelity
World +Sun – worldwide recognition
World+Judgement– receipt of inheritance